"Every time I open a motivational book I want to be inspired. A-Z Blueprint For Success did so in a simple, constructive and unique way. I know I'll implement some of Chris' ideas in both my personal and professional life immediately."

Keith Williams, VP/GM ESPN

"*A-Z Blueprint for Success* is one of the most exciting books of its kind in years. It is packed with powerful concepts, fantastic tips and tricks, and essential information. Chris Vanderzyden's view is completely fresh, enlivening and a must read for all."

Peter Gray, Author of *Pocket Idiot's Guide to Performance Appraisal Phrases and Beyond the Resume*

"Chris challenges us to break the shackles of a reactionary, spiraling existence to be transformed into a content, productive and balanced being."

Paul M. Heinze,
President, Paul M. Heinze Company

"We all want to elevate our lives and A-Z is a wonderful blueprint to guide us to take action and build successful businesses and enhance our lives. A wonderful book for all readers - young and old!"

Karen DeNatale,
President, DeNatale & Associates, Inc.

A person's character thrives when three domains of growth and development are in balance: body, mind and spirit. Care for your body; exercise and feed it well. Stretch your mind and reflect on what you learn. Strengthen your spirit and nurture your soul. Keep things in balance and you will be ready to succeed where life plays out—in your work and in your relationships.

Vanderzyden found herself in a distressingly out-of-balance condition, reflected on its staggering cost and took action. She has reflected on her personal crisis and brought those insights to bear on her work and personal life. In this book, she has organized that hard-won wisdom and serves it up for your consideration in chapters that are bite-sized and stand on their own. It's a provocative read.

-Terry Limpert, Management Consultant

A-Z BLUEPRINT FOR SUCCESS

A Strategy of Action Steps
to Elevate Your Business and Life

Chris Vanderzyden

BALBOA.
PRESS

A DIVISION OF HAY HOUSE

Second Edition

ISBN: 978-1-4525-5359-7 (sc)
ISBN: 978-1-4525-5360-3 (e)
ISBN: 978-1-4525-5361-0 (hc)

Library of Congress Control Number: 2012910321

Balboa Press books may be ordered through booksellers or by contacting:

Balboa Press, A Division of Hay House
1663 Liberty Drive
Bloomington, IN 47403
www.balboapress.com
1-(877) 407-4847

Printed in the United States of America

Balboa Press rev. date: 01/21/13

I dedicate this book, A-Z Blueprint for Success, to all of you who continually strive to lead a successful life. I acknowledge that I have been fortunate to have wonderful teachers in my life who have encouraged and guided me to create a successful life and I wish this book to be a resource to all of you as you build your business and life of success.

CONTENTS

"We are not animals. We are not a product of what has happened to us in our past. We have the power of choice."
—Stephen Covey

A-Z Blueprint for Success

FOREWORD

THE DEFINITION OF SUCCESS is subjective. Whether we want it or recognize it, we have many definitions imposed by our society, our families, our communities, and of course, the organizations or companies that we work for.

You are the only person who can truly define what your personal success is. Once you understand your own clear definition of what constitutes your success, you can strive to reach for success in your personal and professional life.

I started writing this book when I realized my clients didn't understand their success was contingent upon the integration of success in both their personal and professional lives. My clients would work very hard, but then struggle to move forward because they lacked a key skill in one area of their life.

Unfortunately, our personal lives are often negatively infringed upon by our professional lives. While I was working as a CPA for Coopers & Lybrand and then Kenneth Leventhal in Los Angeles, my whole world centered on my professional life. My every day was dictated by an organization's demands, and my success was determined not by me, but by what my bosses felt was successful-how many billing hours I could produce in a given week. Needless to say, this did not meet my own definition of success.

Yes, I was making a nice living, but the expense to my personal life was tremendous. I lived in a smog-filled environment, slogging my way through traffic every day to work at a demanding pace that didn't allow for a personal life. I lived in Los Angeles during the time of the Rodney King riots, the Northridge earthquake, drought, subsequent Malibu fires and mudslides. I also experienced a murder that occurred on my front lawn. It's a gross understatement to say my life was off kilter and unsuccessful.

I realized life was a series of choices rather than a single, dictated event. My success had to include a balance of both the personal and the professional. I took a very drastic step, and my husband and I moved from Los Angeles to a tiny town in Vermont. Moving from a big city to a small town is not for everyone, but for me, the move was an opportunity for balance that allowed me to live a successful life professionally and personally.

Personally, I'm now the mother of two children who are thriving in a safe environment, within a supportive community with great schools and a healthy way of life. I have designed my life so that my family is my main focus. Professionally, after escaping the high-rise buildings and confines of the corporate world, I found my creativity and started an ad specialty and business consulting company. My business affords me a balanced lifestyle to nourish both my professional and personal lives. I have created a life where I am living on my own terms in accordance with my definition of a successful life—and you can too!

I've written this book to guide you in the development of the necessary skills for success in your personal and professional life. I encourage you after each chapter to evaluate your strengths and weaknesses in each area, take action and create a strategy to improve upon the weaknesses while leveraging your strengths. Success is yours with a bit of clarity, effort and strategy.

ESTABLISHING YOUR OWN DEFINITION OF SUCCESS

BEFORE I BEGIN WITH the nuts and bolts of A-Z, I want to discuss the importance of identifying your definition of success. If you don't have a clear vision of how you want to live your life, or what your life looks like according to your own definition of success, then it will be very hard to develop a blueprint of how to get there.

Sometimes it takes a few crashes to realize that the way you are currently living is just not what you truly desire! I had to experience a maddening lifestyle in Los Angeles to clearly identify what I *didn't* want which propelled me forward toward my vision of what I *did* want. In the process, I created my definition of a successful life. In order for your life to be successful, it is necessary for your personal and professional life to be in alignment with your vision.

The first step in the process of developing my vision of success began with settling in and identifying my core values. What mattered most to me would dictate where I spent my time. If you spend your time involved with what resonates with your core values, your life will ultimately be balanced and successful.

If you are not sure where your values lie, look at your checkbook. Sounds funny, doesn't it? If you really want to see where you focus your time, just take a look at how and where you spend your money. Where do the expenditures go? That is an exercise worth performing to find out where your time is going today. Next, honestly evaluate if your expenditure of time and money really supports your core values.

I limit my values to four areas so that I have four quadrants that make up the focus of my life. If my time and money is spent serving one of the four quadrants, then voilá, my life is successful according to me.

Once you have identified your core values, focus all of your time and energy on these areas. Do this, and your life will be in balance, aligned with your life vision and successful by your definition!

I have dedicated the rest of the book to key skills that will help you strive for success in your personal and professional life. I believe we can have it all, and you deserve to have a successful life. It's all a choice, so enjoy the read and make the right choices along the way!

"Attitude is a little thing that makes a big difference."
—Winston Churchill

ATTITUDE

WE HAVE ALL HAD that experience when we are so stressed our attitude can slip from positive to negative in a heartbeat. Those are the moments where we know that our choice of attitude could make or break us. I had one of those moments a few years ago when I was working on a time sensitive project. I was working for a Fortune 100 company and was on vacation and expected to be back furiously working on this project on Monday. I was in London and, unfortunately, the Eyjafjallajokull volcano erupted and stopped all air travel. To further complicate matters, I had given in to my husband's pleas for me to leave my computer and blackberry behind, so that I could truly vacation! Stranded in London with no computer and under client pressure was not the best recipe for a positive attitude. I did have a melt down for a moment before I resolved to take on the challenge with a positive attitude and outsmart the volcano. Believe me, it is much easier to think clearly with a go get 'em attitude! With my positive attitude I marched to the closest Apple store and set up an office in the hotel and for nine days, stranded in London, I remained positive. My client applauded my resolve to stay positive and focused on the project and said, "We couldn't tell you were not in your office".

I speak to organizations about success, motivation, business development, and life balance. I teach how to create a strategy of action that will guide the audience towards leading a life that fulfills their highest potential. The cornerstone of all of these subjects is attitude. Some people have labeled me a motivational speaker. I call myself an educator/trainer, and if people leave the room motivated that is an added bonus. Quite often when I am preparing for an event, my client will frequently ask, "How do we motivate our people?" Motivation has been a question for centuries and studied by researchers extensively. Mark Twain in his much revered novel, *The Adventures of Tom Sawyer*, examines motivation when Tom is assigned the task of whitewashing Aunt Polly's fence. In this chapter, Tom inspires his friends to take over this chore because his attitude presents the task not as work, but play. Our attitude towards a task will ultimately determine our level of motivation.

What truly motivates people to perform?

Independence: The freedom to perform one's work choosing how, when and where. Independence has a profound impact upon attitude.

Having consulted with small business owners and corporations for years, I will say one of the more prominent motivators among the self-employed and employees alike is the desire for control over their own destiny. The freedom to perform work creatively with the ultimate goal of self-satisfaction is a strong motivator. When I worked in the corporate world, I found that employees were much more motivated to perform high quality work when they were given the freedom to do so. They were motivated when they felt empowered and supported and were not constrained by corporate policy. I had an assistant years ago who was pursuing a dream of being a published author of 19th century romantic novels. I encouraged her to utilize her time wisely and work on her personal project at the office with the stipulation that her work for me be completed in a timely fashion. Guess what? Her work was impeccable, and she is now a very successful author with multiple published books. Giving her the freedom to pursue her outside interest created motivation for her to perform in both areas successfully.

Mastering a skill:

Have you ever noticed a child's face as she rolls over for the very first time or takes that very first step, or the attitude exuded by an employee who has succeeded in developing a breakthrough product for a company? Mastery of a skill is an incredible innate motivator. The desire to succeed is in fact how we are hard wired from the beginning. It is human nature to want to put forth effort to obtain a desired result. Excellence or victory is one of the strongest motivators.

Purpose:

Deep motivation is grounded in a profound belief that your actions are serving a higher purpose. Directing our actions toward the improvement of someone or something outside ourselves motivates us to succeed. There are many organizations that move beyond profit and contribute towards a cause as part of their business model. The Orvis Company, a family owned retail and mail-order business specializing in fly fishing, hunting and sporting goods donates five percent of pre-tax profits to conservation projects. Current president, Ray McCready, sites their devotion to providing resources towards conservation as an integral motivator for employees, customers and is one of five core values for the company.

Have you noticed that money is not listed here as a top motivator? Research shows it is perceived only as a "threshold motivator". Compensation only motivates to a point and then the return diminishes substantially once a certain income level is achieved.

Mark Twain's *The Adventures of Tom Sawyer* demonstrates that our attitude has enormous impact upon our level of motivation. The attitude we choose as we travel through life will ultimately determine our level of motivation and dictate our level of success. A positive or a negative attitude is ultimately your choice.

When speaking at a corporate event I can always immediately sense the attitude presented by the participants. A convention for sales professionals stands out in my mind because the energy amongst the 3,000 participants was contagious and quite memorable! Their desire for success was palpable. They gathered with enthusiasm at the hotel, sharing their strategies to get themselves to the next level by next year's corporate event. The company hosting this grand event was presenting new ideas, new products, and integrating training through breakout sessions to fuel their fire. This group demonstrated that their attitude valued achievement as they packed the breakout sessions in order to gain new knowledge to aid them in their progress. They exhibited a steadfast belief in their purpose, and they were truly motivated.

On the plane home I reflected on the positive energy of this event. The common denominator of these successful participants was they all clearly had made the choice of owning a positive **attitude**. Every day we get up and we are afforded the choice: good day or bad day? All of these people seemed to have chosen a good day. Now 3,000 people are considered a lot; it's a swarm, a pack, or gaggle if you will, and a good attitude is contagious in that environment. So I was hopeful, as they all separated at the end of the conference, that the chosen positive attitude present at the conference was carried home to their day-to-day lives. Rest assured, I'm not implying that we should never be allowed a bad day. This is life, after all, and madness happens that tests our ability to hold on to that positive attitude.

Once we have chosen a positive attitude, how do we face our daily challenges?

- **Be sure to start your day doing something you love.** I like to run, as it gets my body moving. I'm always hopeful that if I run far enough, the endorphins will kick in and stay throughout the day. I used to think if I ran faster, that would keep the endorphins flowing. But I recognize I'm just too old to rely on speed anymore, so I go for the basic feel-good goal! You don't have to run. Just start your day doing something you love that will set your day on the right path. And if you have to wake up earlier to squeeze it in, do it. Trust me, you will get used to it and it will set your day up nicely with a positive attitude.

- **Be mindful of the information you take in.**
Read something that inspires you, listen to a CD with a positive message on the way to work, or listen to uplifting music. Be mindful of listening to the news; nothing can kill a positive attitude faster than an earful of bad news over which we have no control.

- **Be sure you choose your friends wisely, deflecting negative energy.**
Remember what your mom would say, "Your friends speak volumes about who you are!" Surround yourself with creative, positive people. We absorb the energy around us, so if we are with negative, chaotic people, our thoughts and actions become negative and chaotic.

- **Be resilient and creative when a challenge presents itself.** Recognize what you can't change, and then move on. If you cannot change something, acknowledge the issue, learn from the situation, and again, simply move on. When you are confronted by a situation that isn't particularly positive, harness your thoughts. A bad situation needn't become a runaway train of negativity. The financial news loves to feed us fear-based information; the Dow Jones is down, and your thoughts swirl to bread lines! Resist indulging in this runaway thinking.

- **Be thankful for your gifts.**
  Gratitude is a great stabilizer. At the end of each day, list all of the positive events that happened, the positive people you encountered, and the challenges you overcame. Then focus your mindset for another great day tomorrow.

The best strategy for success is to choose a positive attitude and keep your motivation at the highest level. Success will then be yours.

Take Action – Attitude is imperative for success, and a positive attitude is a choice. What attitude do you choose and what steps can you take to encourage you to develop and maintain a positive attitude on a daily basis in your life?

"Happiness is not a matter of intensity, but of balance, order, rhythm and harmony."
—Thomas Merton

BALANCE

THE DEFINITION OF BALANCE is flexibility or a state of equilibrium. Balance is the result of one's life in harmony with our core beliefs. It is a state of serenity and a sense that all the parts of our lives are moving in a synergistic way. We are serene and confident in our beliefs and our life actions and habits support our belief system. When we are working in service to our core beliefs, we are at our highest performance. Balance, however, is a moving target, as life is dynamic and we are presented on a daily basis, it seems with challenges that threaten our balance. Today we see people with demanding careers, caring for a family, caring for elderly parents, volunteering in their community. The list of roles is endless, and multitasking is a way of life. Technology can often compound the problem, as we are easily accessible and distracted thanks to email, cell phones, and the Internet.

Work/life balance is one of the biggest challenges that employers and employees continually face on a continuous basis, an issue that threatens productivity and the health of companies and employees alike. The Society for Human Resource Management (SHRM) conducted a study of American work-life balance in 2010 and revealed the following statistics:

- Among the 89 percent of Americans who say work/life balance is a problem, 54 percent called it a "significant" problem.
- 57 percent of workers think that their employer is doing enough to address work/life balance issues; 43 percent do not.
- 38 percent of workers say their work/life balance has worsened because of the recession.
- 37 percent of those who do not have adequate balance say time with family is the first thing that suffers; personal time spent reading or relaxing followed, at 22 percent.
- 44 percent of men ages 34-54 say they do not have adequate work/life balance.

When I was living in Los Angeles, my life was completely unbalanced and focused in one area of value: my professional life. I was simply unhappy and living an unsuccessful life. My first move towards balance was physically moving to an environment that I knew I could thrive in. For me that meant moving across country, but it does not have to be a drastic upheaval. Don't be a victim of your self-created circumstance. You can choose to take action and create the environment that works for you, fostering an improved work/life balance. Today, I still struggle to balance my four quadrants of values, but I make a conscious decision to focus every day and keep myself in check.

A clear set of balance strategies implemented daily will overcome the challenge of establishing balance.

- **Establish Priorities.**

  Narrow your focus to those four core value areas that we spoke about previously. I use my private time while I exercise to revisit my focus areas and evaluate whether I am balanced in where I spend my time. My four quadrants are: family, friends, health, and business. Every moment of my day goes to one of the quadrants and I try to limit intrusions. I encourage you to take time alone and identify four focus points. Once you have identified what is really important to you based on your values, everything you do and choose should serve only these four focus areas. Invest your time, energy and money on what is important to you. I have included in Appendix A, a list of values that will guide you in identifying your priorities.

- **Edit your life.**

  What worked yesterday or last year doesn't mean that it is working today. Be an active participant in your life and get rid of people or activities that don't support your focus points or bring negativity or chaos into your life. I have left friends, clients and activities behind when they have ceased to be positive contributors. I've never regretted my choices and it always creates space for more positive things to be introduced.

- **Manage your time.**

  Organization is the key to optimal time management. We all need to maximize our time in order to balance our life and organizing your time so as not to be wasteful is a necessity. Block out times for specific activities and avoid disruption as much as possible. I schedule my day in blocks based on skill. I have my creative time, communication and meeting time and administrative time. By clustering specific activities together, I am more productive.

Also, we all are, from time to time, confronted with people who are energy sinks. Make a conscious decision as to whom you allow into your space and how you spend your time. Be aware of mindless activities that can burn time, such as incessantly reading email. I do not have my email set for automatic download; I decide when I check my emails. Evade the time gobblers!

- **Focus on wherever you are.**

  The ability to focus is key to maintaining a life of balance. This is really hard at times, but turn off that cell phone every now and then. When you are with your family, be with your family; when you're at work, be at work. I have a 5-foot rule in business, meaning that when I am working I will speak to anyone within five feet about my business. However, when I am with family, the 5-foot rule goes out the window and I don't divide my attention.

- **Set your boundaries.**

  Learn to say "No." It is such a simple one-syllable word, and yet we have so much trouble at times saying it. When I am approached with an invitation or request, even if I know that I definitely want to say yes, I always say, "I need to check my calendar and I will get back to you." I do this so that I can go away and decide whether the event or activity is something I really want to do and serves one of my focus areas.

- **Accept help.**

  Identify when you need help, who can provide it, and then accept it. Too many times we seem to try to do it all and suffer from martyr syndrome. It is okay to say "uncle" every now and then and pull in some outside troops to help carry the load. We all have tremendous responsibilities and we cannot be successful without outside help. For my entrepreneurial clients, I advise them to hire anyone who can perform a task for you for less than $100.00. This policy will ensure that you are best utilizing your talents.

> **Take Action** – *Identify your four value quadrants. Analyze how balanced your life is and implement an effective strategy to help you maintain your balance.*

"Communication is a skill that you can learn. It's like riding a bicycle or typing. If you're willing to work at it, you can rapidly improve the quality of every part of your life" —**Brian Tracy**

COMMUNICATION

EFFECTIVE COMMUNICATION IS PROFOUNDLY important to our personal and professional success. Our style of communication and our ability to listen is the key to developing and sustaining our relationships, and our success is determined in large part by our relationships. Communication poses the most challenges in all areas of our lives, but it is a skill that can be easily improved with knowledge and practice.

Think about all of the people with whom you communicate in a given day, and how many times you modify your communications in accordance with your audience. We change the way we communicate according to demographics, whether we are speaking to a man, a women or a child. We also change the style we use to convey a message based on the mode of communication: the telephone, writing, public speaking, or face-to-face. The flexibility required to effectively communicate is enormous, and fortunately we have ample opportunities posed daily to improve this skill!

Effective communication is pivotal to the success of any business organization. Whether it is in internal communications or customer relations, our style and method will determine how our message is received and if we have produced the intended results.

Communicating with the goal of business development has become more efficient than ever thanks to the myriad of communication options available today. Technology has made it far easier to communicate with our customers and collect data on the needs of our customers, which have increased our ability to satisfy our customers' desires. With our phones, tablets, computers, face time and social media, we have a seemingly endless array of options with which to communicate. All of this opportunity has created an ever-increasing amount of communication, so our challenge is to create a message that won't get filtered out.

Our opportunity to get our "point" across is shrinking at an ever-increasing pace as people are inundated with communication. Today audience's attention span has been reduced drastically as they struggle to decipher and accept or delete communication. There is pressure to grab our audience's attention quickly. Whether we are speaking to a client, prospective customer, employee or waiter, our articulation needs to be quick and concise in order for our message to be heard.

Jeffrey Hayzlett, in his bestselling book *Running the Gauntlet*, gives the advice that your pitch to a potential customer needs to be done in 118 seconds. Eight seconds to grab the attention of your prospect and one hundred and ten seconds to reel them in!

He suggests after grabbing your prospect's attention in eight seconds relaying the following in the remaining one hundred and ten seconds:

- Convey who you are
- Describe what your business offers
- Explain the promises you will deliver upon

The goal is to present your idea or product in an enticing and clear manner in less than two minutes, because your listener's attention span is just that short. Your message needs to inform, entertain and create a connection with your audience on an emotional or personal level in order to convince your listener to take action.

The development of any relationship begins with clear, effective communication. Whether you're developing a sales team, selling a product or opportunity, or interacting in your personal life, your success ultimately hinges on how well and relevantly you communicate the message to your audience.

Here is a guideline to develop a purposeful and productive sales conversation:

- **Check on your mindset before you begin your conversation.**
  Are you feeling positive and confident about your opportunity or product and the solution you are offering to a prospect's challenge? Your confidence should convince the listener that he or she is fortunate to be hearing about your opportunity. Be aware that if you are too eager or seem desperate to "sell" your product or idea, your listener will sense this and you risk immediate rejection.

- **Build rapport with your prospect.**
  Ask a question that is related to the situation that brought you in contact with that person. This will establish a mutual connection. Be authentic by presenting your true self. This will establish

trust, which is the key ingredient to successful relationships in business, just as it is in your personal life. Always remember that people buy from people whom they know and trust.

- **Introduce yourself and your business.**
  Expand upon yourself, your experience, and how your opportunity has had a positive impact. This is your opportunity to build credibility and to differentiate yourself from your competition. Let your prospect know why you are better than everyone else.

- **Ask open and expanding questions**.
  Allow the person the opportunity to explain his or her current situation, challenges and goals. Listen to the prospect's answers, ask more questions, and reiterate your understanding of what he or she says. We'll discuss the importance of perfecting your active listening skills in a forthcoming chapter.

- **Summarize your understanding of the situation**.
  Present how your opportunity provides a solution to your prospect's needs. Be very specific about how what you are offering is the resolution to their problem. For example: "I believe that our product will increase productivity and revenue by 20% in the first year of implementation".

- **Conclude your conversation.**
  Set up the next meeting or phone call with a specific day and time.

On a final note, if the end result of your conversation is that your prospect is not interested, be gracious, thankful for the conversation, and move on quickly. There is always someone else who needs to hear your message, and time is precious.

> ***Take Action** – Develop your opening pitch or 118 as Jeff Hayzlett discusses. Consistently evaluate your communication style and sharpen your skills to increase your success.*

"Discipline is the refining fire by which
talent becomes ability."
—Roy L. Smith

DISCIPLINE

THE TEN THOUSAND HOUR Rule. Yes, according to many experts including Malcolm Gladwell, the author of *The Tipping Point, Blink* and *Outliers: The Story of Success*, it requires approximately 10,000 hours to become proficient at a new skill. Whether it is learning to play the piano, learning a new sport, or developing a new business, it's a pretty large commitment of time! The only way to reach this lofty goal is to be disciplined in your practice. Persistence and passion for the desired skill are also key factors.

Passion + Persistence + Discipline = Success

Discipline is the key ingredient in this equation. I am a runner, and frequently when I am getting out of my cozy warm bed on cold dark mornings, strapping on my running sneakers, I hear the same old recording in my mind, "Why, why, why?"! Then, of course, the answer comes to me: **Discipline gets me to success.** Now, everyone who has watched me run knows that I am a turtle running down the road, but I am out there. In the end, *the discipline of running translates to discipline in my personal and professional life.* Having the self-control to push myself to get up every morning to run sets my focus for the day. It serves me personally and then the benefit rolls forward into my professional life to help me achieve my goals every day.

Discipline is self-control, and it is the key to productivity. It's the ability to maintain your focus and applying consistent effort in improving a skill in order to reach your success. Discipline requires that you identify a regimen that will support each of your goals. Don't procrastinate. Figure out what your goals are and the skills you need to develop in order to reach your goals. Apply consistent effort, and you will reach your success.

I categorize discipline into three elements: *mental, emotional* and *physical*. In order to achieve success, it is necessary that our discipline be focused in all of the areas, both professionally and personally, in order to be truly effective leaders.

- **Mental Discipline**.
  The ability to maintain your focus when distractions are present. It is the ability to keep your focus on whatever task you're performing so that you do it well. It is mastering the art of being present in the moment, which allows us to function effectively and efficiently.

*Tip: Manage your work environment so that your interruptions are kept to a minimum. Write a list of the day's activities and focus on each in turn. Schedule each task, such as checking email, at specific times so that you are not being interrupted incessantly.

- **Emotional Discipline.**
  The ability to prevent runaway thoughts and control your negative emotions and feelings threatening to derail you from focused positive intention. It is the talent to make thoughtful choices that serve your core values

Tip: Recognize that you choose your feelings about any given situation. Don't give way to destructive emotions. Harness run-away thoughts.

- **Physical Discipline.**
  The ability to nurture your physical wellbeing. It is the ability to make yourself do something, when you should do it, whether you want to or not.

Tip: Make taking care of yourself a routine and a priority. Set aside a specific time to exercise, and then do it. Track your progress. I've kept a running log for years and it keeps me disciplined to practice every day and see my results.

When you are feeling tired, discouraged-ready to throw in the towel-apply discipline! You will almost always break through to achievement.

> **Take Action –** *Institute a conscious mindset of discipline in your daily life.*

"Enthusiasm is excitement with inspiration, motivation, and a pinch of creativity."
—Bo Bennett

ENTHUSIASM

THERE IS NO DOUBT that some people are enthusiastic by nature. I have been accused from time-to-time of possessing a high level of enthusiasm and, at times, I have even been accused of flat-out overzealousness. But I do believe that my high level of expectation or enthusiasm has served me well! **Enthusiasm creates momentum**, but if the enthusiasm is not authentic, it is immediately detectable by those around us; that has a genuinely negative impact on our conversations.

On the flip side, if there is no enthusiasm at all, then that is just trouble. For instance, I have been to many networking events where I have encountered someone presenting their business with no enthusiasm at all. Yawn. I mean, really, if you are taking the time to present, please bring some enthusiasm with you-just a little something to capture my attention. I'm not saying you have to be a rock star, but honestly, do you think you will inspire with drab? It is frustrating to listen to someone present with no excitement and no inspiration.

What is the power of enthusiasm? Well, if you don't love what you do, if you don't have the energy to inspire, you will not be successful. Simply move on and find another avenue. If there is no enthusiasm, then it is just work. And when what we are pursuing is work, it's impossible to perform at our best. **It is imperative that your love for the game shines through in every conversation, so that you will inspire your audience to take action.**

If you exude enthusiasm, it will be contagious and you'll find that others in your organization will follow — and thus success! Have you ever been around someone with a great laugh, a "yuckel" of a laugh, and even if they are laughing at something that just isn't funny, you still laugh? That is an infectious laugh, and enthusiasm is the same: infectious.

If we love what we do, then shouldn't we be really enthusiastic and infect the people around us? I'm not talking about the flu here. Let's just grab everyone with our enthusiasm and move him or her towards success with us. **If you are developing a team, selling an idea or a product, your enthusiasm-or lack of it-will shine through, creating a positive or negative outcome.**

I understand that maintaining a high level of enthusiasm can be challenging. When the chips are down, when you've hit a wall, when there seem to be more no's than yes's, when your message isn't being heard and the frustration is high, don't despair.

Here are a few regrouping tactics to get you going again:

- **Know the reason why.**
  Do you really know why you are working so hard? If you can answer that question and have a clear vision of why you are striving to reach your goals your enthusiasm for the process should not wane. I sometimes go for days on end with just a dream in my head replaying over and over. Realistic or not, my focus on the dream increases my enthusiasm. Use a vision board. Envision your passion in a screen saver. Keep your "why" front and center.

- **Be disciplined in your approach and attitude.**
  When fatigue truly sets in, and that does occur from time to time, then it is time to take stock of where you are and how far you have moved forward towards your goals. When we take the time to reflect upon our successes, it will motivate and create renewed enthusiasm to make additional gains.

- **Shake the day up.**
  When the routine begins to tap your enthusiasm, it is time to break the mold. I recommend learning something new. You can take online courses, read a book, or research a new business strategy on the web. When we implement a new strategy or habit into our lives, enthusiasm returns.

- **Reboot.**
  If you notice your glass is half full and your enthusiasm wanes, you may simply need rest. We cannot maintain our productivity or enthusiasm without taking the time to recharge. All work and no play are bad for business and your personal relationships. When you are rested you will find that new ideas come to mind more readily and your zest for your business and life will quickly return.

Enthusiasm is also a great resource to reduce the fear of striving for something new. It makes you blindly go where you would normally not, and that is often a good thing!

Take Action – Refresh, regroup and find that energy and passion for whatever it is you do!

"Money isn't the most important thing in life, but it's reasonably close to oxygen on the 'gotta have it' scale."
- Zig Ziglar

FISCAL RESPONSIBILITY

PEOPLE FEAR MONEY. HOW many of you reading this book experience incessant negative thoughts regarding money? People fear that if they don't have money today they will never have money in the future. If they do have money, they are fearful that they will lose their money. I have clients, an elderly couple, who have millions and millions invested; yet, they focus on and worry about losing their money every day. They were born during the Great Depression, and I am confident their fear is rooted in their childhood memories of scarcity. It is incredibly sad that they waste time guarding their money when in reality; their money will last for generations and generations. I grew up in a large family during the 70's, and I have lasting memories of the energy crisis and inflation. My father was even laid off. My attitude and fear early in life of money or lack of money certainly came from those experiences in my developmental years.

My career choice as a Certified Public Accountant reflected that fear. Obtaining my CPA license basically meant that I took a humongous three-day exam and toughed out a few years working for Coopers & Lybrand in public accounting during my twenties. After working in public accounting and then as an asset manager in Los Angeles, I made the journey into marketing and my current life as an entrepreneur. I was competent as a CPA, but it was not my passion or bliss but an attempt to control my fear of poverty. Knowledge is power! My success as an entrepreneur was made easier because of my roots in finance and being diligent in continuing to obtain financial knowledge. You don't need to be a CPA to take control of your finances. However, you do need to be disciplined in your approach to the management of your finances.

The truth is, it won't matter a hill of beans if you make money in your business if you don't have a clue as to what to do with the moolah once it comes along. We have all seen it, we've heard it, and a few have lived the big financial success followed by the deafening crash. It takes discipline to grow a business and even more discipline to protect the rewards.

Generally, it takes about five years to launch a business and really begin to see the financial rewards. While developing your business, it is important to watch your pennies and continue to invest in yourself and your business.

Now when you have started to make money, here are a few simple money management guidelines:

- **Set your financial goals.**
  You should do this monthly, yearly, every three years, and every five years. Once you have your goals set, clearly define your strategy to get there. Understand your income and expenses and your long-term and short-term debts. People talk about good debt and bad debt.

An example of "good" debt would be a mortgage. It's considered good debt because mortgage interest is tax deductible and owning a home was meant to hedge against inflation. You could have a mortgage at a low interest rate, and rather than use funds to fully pay off the mortgage, you could focus your money on investments at higher yield rates, such as the stock market. This is considered by some to be a positive financial strategy. An example of bad debt is, of course, credit card debt.

In today's uncertain economic environment, *good debt is a myth*. In order to achieve financial success, you must erase all of your debt and then strategically invest in *income producing assets*.

Recognize that when you are starting a business, **you must invest in your business with time and money**. It takes time to recoup the initial investment, and it takes great courage to have the faith that your financial investment will pay dividends, so institute an attitude of confidence and faith.

- **Budget.**

    Sorry, very boring. But yes, you should have a budget in place for your business and for your personal life. Do the work and write down all of your income sources and expenses. Also, don't forget to make a line item for taxes (our biggest obligation), especially if you are a small business owner. There is no better motivation to create income when you have all of your expenses and liabilities staring you in the face. Once you have your budget defined, be disciplined and stick to it. Review your budget regularly and hold yourself accountable. Sacrifice and hard work are the driving forces behind financial success.

I advise people to carry a pad of paper for one week and write down everything you spend money on. At the end of the week, review this piece of paper. It's a great representation of where you're spending your money, where you're leaking money, and where you need to become more disciplined to avoid extravagant expenditures.

- **Be a good example for your children.**
  Most public school systems teach zero in regards to financial responsibility. So teach your children about finances and set a good example. A few strategies to teach your children about finance include:

1. Set up a checking account for them while they are in high school and have them use their tech savvy to set up the account in Quicken or some other money management computer system. Set up a Roth IRA for them.
2. Teach them about investing and the difference between passive, active and portfolio income.
3. Teach them how to budget and how to plan for retirement.
4. Teach them what debt is, how taxes affect them, and what inflation is.

Knowledge is power. Our future generation's success hinges on their understanding of money. Show them how to develop a positive attitude rather than a fearful one toward money. Teach them and teach them well.

- **Share, Contribute, Tithe.**

  Last but not least, don't forget to share, contribute, and/or tithe. Giving is tax deductible and is simply the right thing to do! But let's also look at one of the best investors in the world, Warren Buffet. In 2006 alone, he gave $1.9 billion to charities and pledged to grow that exponentially over the next 20 years. Sometimes we just aren't in the position to give money, so give your time to an organization instead, as it is important to give back to our communities. A longer, happier, healthier life has been attributed to those who give more.

Your attitude towards money, whether it is a fear of abundance or a fear of scarcity, is strong indicator of your potential for success. We all struggle with fear in our lives. How we choose to work with our fear will determine our success in our businesses and our personal lives.

Fear is a powerful hindrance to progress. We cannot reach our goals with fear as an anchor, whether we are striving to move our business to a new level, lose weight or live an authentic life. Fear can be, if allowed, an insurmountable force that creates resistance to change.

I love this acronym:

FEAR = FALSE EVIDENCE APPEARING REAL

When working with business clients, I frequently ask them to tell me what exactly they feel they need to do, something that they are not currently doing, which will make them more successful. A very simple question and frequently they will tell me in a split second what they are not doing and from there we quickly peel back the layers and identify the underlying fear that keeps them from moving forward. There is frequently one action that will make all of the difference in the world to the success of their business. Once we have identified the root of their fear, we can then implement a strategy to move forward.

Here are a few strategies to help you to move forward beyond the fear that binds you to inaction towards achieving your goals:

- **Identify your fear**.
  Fear lets you know that you are going to make a change, and you may not understand the end result. The unknown is fearful for most people. Identify exactly what the fear is. Maybe it is a fear of failure, or maybe a fear of success itself, or a fear of rejection. Simply pay attention to your internal dialogue as to why you can't do something and find the core of your fear.

When I hear clients say "I'm afraid" that is when I really start cheering, as I know they are in the process of identifying their fear and on their way to taking action. First step toward success; identify the fear-whatever it is that keeps you in a stagnant position.

- **Embrace your fear.** Ask yourself, "What is the worst possible outcome?" 90% of what we worry about never happens. So worrying about failure, or the result of your success is senseless and a waste of time. If the worst outcome you imagine does indeed happen, then worrying about that scenario afforded you the fearful experience not once, but twice, once with worry and a second time when it actually happens! Don't waste time worrying about the ugly, unreal scenario that your mind has conjured up. I don't believe we can *overcome* our fears, but I do believe we can take the necessary action to work through our fears to move forward. Embrace your fears, create a rock solid strategy to work through them and bravely implement your strategy.

- **Choose Action.** Understand that fear can be useful. Fear will make you pause to really think through your strategy. Being fearless can be detrimental and downright scary. Fearlessness can cause you to move forward when you should not, so utilize the fear to get clear on your strategy and then jump into the change.

In the end the choice to accept the risk, take action and live your life to your true potential is all up to you. We all have power over our lives, and it is up to you to utilize your power and identify your fear, choose to embrace your fear and take action or not.

Many successful people have had huge failures prior to their success. Fear of failure is often the common denominator of all of our fears. ***Success, however, is just a compilation*** *of our failures, and every time you fail you are closer to success.*

Henry Ford: We all know his great innovation was the assembly line that changed American manufacturing, but Ford failed at multiple businesses before he succeeded.

Bill Gates: The king of Microsoft failed at his first business Traf-O-Data. I am willing to bet he learned quickly from that deal and never repeated the mistakes he made.

Oprah Winfrey: Yes, even Oprah failed, and was fired from one of her earlier jobs.

Don't be afraid of failure. Our success is the culmination of all that we have learned when we have failed. Every step forward includes risk and some risk is unforeseen. Those steps, even if we deemed them a failure, are part of the road to success if you learn from the failure, adjust and move on quickly.

So fail hugely. Take a risk and succeed or fail big-I mean really big, huge, going down in flames big. When I hear about big failures, I know that huge successes are on the way, so embrace your fear and go for it – either way you will succeed.

Fiscal responsibility requires that you take control of your finances and your attitudes towards money and refuse to allow fear to get in the way. As Zig Ziglar says, "Money isn't the most important thing in life, but it's reasonably close to oxygen on the 'gotta have it' scale.", so you might as well embrace the function of money, understand it and take responsibility for it.

Take Action – *Review your attitude towards money (are you fearful?) and develop a strategy to invite more money into your life. Write (yes I mean pen to paper or click away on your computer) a full money strategy. What are your financial goals? What is your strategy to achieve those goals? What is your investment strategy? Create an annual budget.*

"Goals in writing are dreams with deadlines."
—Brian Tracy

A-Z Blueprint for Success

GOALS

I LOVE THIS QUOTE from Brian Tracy. Doesn't it inspire action? I find that most of my clients, me included, respond very well to goal setting because it formulates an action plan and without a plan, it is easy to settle into complacency. I, myself, would be completely adrift without having carefully thought out goals and strategies. I would be listing aimlessly through life without any clear direction. If you are very clear on what your dreams are and take the time to create a series of small goals to move you to that end result, your rate of success will skyrocket.

Setting goals is a tool that will aid you in realizing what you aspire to become. Our lives are comprised of a series of choices. Which path we choose is up to us, and the end result will be the culmination of our goals and the effort we put forth to reach those goals.

The success of our personal lives feeds our success in our professional lives, and vice versa. The *interdependence* of our personal and professional lives is why our goals need to encompass both personal and professional goals. Our lives are hectic, but it is important to do the work and take the time to define your goals and map a specific strategy to achieve them.

Here are a few tips on setting your goals:

- **Identify the 4 focus points of your life.**
  What are the four core values that are important to you? My focus points are *family*, *business*, *health* and *friendships*. Once you have established your four most important values, self reflect and evaluate where you have succeeded and where you have failed in each of these categories. Using these failures and successes, think about where you are today and where you want to be, and then write down your goals. Your goals need to reflect your values. I have included in Appendix A a list of values to help you in establishing your top four core values. A very common reason for stagnation is that we are not focused. If you live your life with intent and every action serves one of your core values, you will experience success in your personal and professional life.

True success will remain out of reach without the proper planning. I recommend setting yearly professional and personal goals, and then breaking the goals down into monthly, weekly, and then a daily *expectation list*.

- **Be sure your goals are S.M.A.R.T.**
  Specific – The more specific you are, the higher the chances you will achieve the true result you desire. When you identify your specific goal, answer the questions of who, what, when, where, why. Who needs to be involved in accomplishing what you

intend to accomplish? What are you specifically going to do? When do you need to succeed? Where does this goal occur? Why is it important to do now? How are you going to accomplish the goal?

Measurable - Your goals should clearly dictate some form of measurement. Dollars, pounds, inches, percent are examples of creating a measurable result. A concrete method to measure your progress will allow you to know when you have actually succeeded. For example, I would like to increase sales by 20%.

Attainable – All goals need to be aligned with your ability, skill level, and financial capacity. For example, becoming a rock star if you are tone deaf is not within your ability. Your goals must be realistic. *It is attainable if you develop the strategy to support the goal and it makes sense.* Your goals must be "doable." Sometimes I set "soft" daily goals so that I have a guaranteed feeling of immediate accomplishment; this gives me the fuel to move on toward the more challenging goals of the day. Soft goals are not necessarily easy goals. It is important that our goals stretch us. If your goal is not even remotely attainable, then you're setting yourself up for failure. The goal should be hard enough that it allows for that "aha!" accomplished feeling when you have met it.

Relevant - Your goals must have impact upon your overall life strategy. They need to resonate with your core values and be pertinent to your definition of a successful life. This is critical. If your goals are not relevant to your life, but you are setting the goal for someone else then you will not be inspired toward achievement. You must own your goal. For instance, you decided to become a professional golfer to please your golf pro grandfather. Let's face it-you are a talented but uninspired golfer. You set this goal just because you know he would love it if you followed in his footsteps. You are setting yourself up for failure because the goal is not relevant to you.

Time bound - Your goals need a deadline so that you have a point of reevaluation. On a daily, weekly, monthly, yearly basis, take the time to evaluate where you are and what steps need to be taken in order to maintain your focus and move towards accomplishing your goals.

- **Reward yourself.**
  As you write down your goals, be sure to include a reward for meeting each goal. Then be sure to actually do it and reward yourself when each goal is reached. It will keep you motivated to move past the pain of work and keep you focused on the end result.

In order to reach your goals, you cannot sit as a spectator but must **take action.** Execution is the key to reaching goals. For each goal, have a **step-by-step strategy in place to support the goal**. Break each goal down into manageable portions so that you have a blueprint to get you to your end point. While creating your strategy include for each step in your strategy every possible challenge and obstacle that could derail your progress. You will come upon a diversion. You will be distracted. You will meet a stumbling block that may trick you into thinking that you cannot go forward. Have the foresight to include all of these roadblocks in your strategy, so that when you come upon them you have a strategy in place to move forward. Be prepared to achieve. Get a coach to help you stay focused. Summon a friend to be accountable to, as you both strive to reach your goals. I am also a proponent of telling everyone about your goals. It is much harder to advertise your desires and then admit failure, so if shame works for you, announce to everyone your intent and then don't let them down!

> *Take Action* – *Set monthly, quarterly, and annual goals. Create a very specific and supporting strategy. Be proactive in routinely evaluating your progress and refining your strategy as you progress.*

"Health is a state of complete harmony of the body, mind and spirit. When one is free from physical disabilities and mental distractions, the gates of the soul open."
—B.K.S. Iyengar

HEALTH

MAINTAINING OUR HEALTH SEEMS a simple task, doesn't it? We all know what we should and shouldn't do, yet somehow we still don't pay complete attention. We make a few bad choices along the way. Our lives are busy, and between our jobs, caring for children, elderly parents, contributing to our communities, etc., we seem to put taking care of ourselves last on the list. In reality we need to be front and center and take care of ourselves so that we are able to give fully to the other people in our lives.

It is true that if we don't take the time to keep ourselves healthy today, we will be forced to take time to be sick later.

So if we are going to have to choose where to spend our time, it is best to choose the healthy route and take time today and every day to be healthy. In order to be effective in caring for others, it is imperative that we first take care of ourselves. If we are depleted emotionally and physically, we cannot take care of others. Have you ever been on a plane with your children and the safety guidelines insist that you put your oxygen mask on first, prior to helping your children and others? It goes against every instinct we feel, doesn't it? Giving yourself the oxygen first will give you the necessary means to help others. It is counterintuitive for us to help ourselves first. However, it is imperative to be strong enough to help others.

Our health is comprised of our spiritual, mental and physical wellbeing. Here are a few thoughts to help you maintain *your* health:

- **Spiritual Health:** Our spiritual health has profound impact on our mental and physical health. If we are vacant spiritually, our mental and physical health is threatened and illness a frequent result. *When we are connected spiritually, our thoughts, words and actions are in alignment. We are then honoring our true self and purpose in life.* Spiritual health brings strength, peace and comfort. We need to nurture our spirituality continuously by staying connected to our true selves. You may do this in a variety of ways, such as meditating, finding refuge in nature, or through your religion. Taking time to stay spiritually connected will help you cope with life's challenges and will improve your overall health.

Challenge

Take two 3-minute time periods this week and focus on your spiritual growth. Enjoy quiet time, meditate, go for a walk in nature... do something to refill your spiritual cup.

- **Mental Health:** Maintaining your mental fitness requires balancing your emotions, maintaining a positive attitude, and striving to improve intellectually.

  1. Discipline your emotions. We all choose how we emotionally react to every situation.

  2. Keep a positive attitude and keep in mind that old saying that every negative has a positive liner somewhere inside. I love that saying!

  3. Exercise your intellectual health. Stay current with events, new technology, and do activities that stretch you out of your comfort zone.

Challenge

Take an hour this week to explore and discover something that isn't directly involved with work. Go to an art showing, visit a museum, read a book that isn't business-related, or watch an educational show.

- **Physical Health:**
  Our physical health encompasses eating well, exercising, and of course, checking in with a doctor from time to time. There are a million guidelines out there that can confuse anybody. Remember the "don't eat eggs" warning of the '90s? Now they are the perfect protein and we should eat them as much as we want!

  1. I encourage you to just do everything in moderation. I use the 20/80 rule for business and food, too. This rule means that what I do 80% of the time has the most impact, so I'll be very focused on that 80%, and be unconcerned with the remaining 20%. So if I have a ton of carbs on Thanksgiving Day, it doesn't concern me in the least.

  2. Exercise consistently. I am a big believer in a good dose of fresh air and movement every day, do whatever you love, just please do it!

Take Action – Honor yourself and the lives that you touch, and care for yourself deeply by keeping yourself healthy; mentally, physically and spiritually. Keep a daily journal of self care. A journal will help you to reflect on how well you are doing in caring for yourself and ultimately the other people in your life.

"Invest in yourself - if you have confidence in yourself."
—William Feather

INVEST

YOU PROBABLY THINK BECAUSE of my finance background I'm going to write about investing your money in this chapter. I discussed the importance of financial investing in the chapter on Fiscal Responsibility; however, in this chapter I am referring to investing in *you*. We are so geared towards evaluating our success by our balance sheet, investment statements and bank account, but truly your greatest asset is yourself. As William Feather states, if you have confidence in yourself, you need to invest in yourself. Many a client has given me detailed reasons, or shall I say excuses, as to why they cannot invest in themselves to achieve success. Most of these excuses involve shortage of time or lack of money.

Every goal I have ever aspired to accomplish, whether personal or professional, has been achieved by an intense investment of time. Frequently, achievement also requires the investment of money. When I was growing up my father would say that investing in an education was the best thing you could do because you could have everything taken away, but nobody could ever take away your knowledge. Time and money invested in knowledge will never be a waste.

So, yes indeed, when you look at the balance sheet of life; houses, children, spouses, investments, careers, mortgages, car payments, taxes, it all centers on you. You are your biggest asset.

You are the one that makes the wheel turn. Without investing in yourself eventually you will rust, and the wheel will stop.

Personally we invest in ourselves when we take care of our health and relationships. Ultimately, our happiness depends on our health and the friends and family with which we surround ourselves. We become unbalanced if we focus only on our professional lives and pay no attention to what truly brings us personal happiness.

Invest your time in developing and maintaining your relationships and invest your money in programs that further your personal goals. Whether a gym membership or a self-development course, a financial investment will keep you, your most important asset, functioning at an optimal level.

Professionally, it is wise to be very astute in how we invest our time and money to further the success of our business. I frequently will ask my clients when we plan each strategy, "What is your ROI (Return on Investment)?" Yes, that is the CPA in me. I love it when someone can just throw a number at me and say, "Chris, I know if I spend x dollars I will get a return of y." Yes, I love that, but the reality is, *sometimes an ROI can't be computed, and we need to quiet the inner chatter of fear, make a leap of faith, and invest in our business with our money and time in order to succeed.*

Reaching success in your business, as well as in your personal life, requires a synergy of time and money.

- **Money:**
  The old adage is true that we must spend money to make money. Invest wisely in areas that create efficiencies and allow for expansion in your business.

There are many businesses that fail because they are either unwilling to invest at all into their business or they have invested unwisely with no strategic plan in place. Create a worthy plan and make the investment. Do this correctly, and the rewards will outweigh the cost.

This year, where will you invest your money to create the return in your business that will provide your business with the success it deserves?

- **Time:**
  Invest in developing relationships that will inspire you and complement your business. So much of our focus goes into the task or the process we use to get results in our business. In fact, many of our conflicts and areas of growth happen around having the *right* relationships with people, and it requires time to nurture those relationships.

Time is really just the effort put forth to convert creativity into money, which then ultimately buys you more valuable time.

In the end, there must be a balance in your time and money investment.

> ***Take Action*** *– Work daily to make sure you are balancing the growth of your finances with the growth of your talent and skills. Create a plan of investment in yourself and in your business.*

"Joy is the umbrella for life's storms."
—Chris Vanderzyden

JOY

I LOVE TO ASK my clients, "What are you doing on a daily basis to bring joy into your life?" The look on their faces as they stammer to give me an answer is priceless. It is often a look of disbelief that A.) They are responsible for bringing joy into their lives and B.) That, yes, they are deserving of joy on a daily basis. Adults seem to feel that only children have a right to joy, but joy is for adults, too!

When I was living in Los Angeles, I felt an enormous lack of joy. My surroundings were not conducive to a joyful life, and without joy I was left feeling depleted and defeated. If we don't have joy in our lives, what is the point? Joy is integral to a successful life, and it all begins with making a conscious choice to live a life that is aligned with your core value system. When I decided to choose to live a life away from Los Angeles and the stressful treadmill of that career, that emotion of delight crept in.

In addition to living a life aligned with our core values, **joy** is also contingent on our thought processes. The great thing about this is that only we get to choose our thoughts, so we have complete control over the outcome of every situation. Align your life with your core values, choose your thoughts wisely, and welcome the joy into your life.

In order to welcome more joy into your life align your life with your core values and focus your thoughts in a positive fashion diligently every day. It is necessary that to make a conscious choice in the way you live your life, you need to give yourself space and time. We fail to stop long enough to evaluate where we are and what we want, and then we let the joy slip away with our unconscious way of life. Take time to choose.

Create the joy you deserve in life. As I previously stated, you alone are responsible for bringing happiness into your life and you deserve it. How do we create joy in our daily life?

- **Acknowledge that you deserve to be joyful.**
  Give yourself permission to be joyful. Unfortunately, our culture believes that working hard with no downtime is to be commended, and relaxing and creating joy is child's play. Reject this notion, and embrace the joy that presents itself. The more you expect this emotion to be evoked, the more often it will appear.

- **The little things in life bring us the most joy.**
  Walking through the woods, watching the clouds, counting the stars. When was the last time your chased a firefly on a hot humid night?

- **Bring joy to someone; it will bring joy to you.**
  I have a daily goal of doing something unexpected for someone else. Because I expect to help someone every day, the opportunity to do so is often presented and it doesn't have to be a huge event, but something simple. I can help an elderly person get out of the car at the grocery store, and we both feel more joyful. You will receive what you give.

- **Take a cue from a child.**
  Every night I ask my girls, "What was the best part of your day? What was the worst part of your day? What

was the funniest part of your day?" Not only does this give me a temperature read on their struggles, but it also sheds light on what brings them joy.

- **Make every day, mundane tasks joyful.**
  Routine tasks can be joyful if you choose to receive joy from the task. For instance, I like to wash dishes on a cold night because it keeps my hands warm. I like feeding the cats because they nuzzle you out of the way of the dish, and that makes me laugh. I like folding clothes fresh out of the dryer, again because they are warm. When I have a complication in my work day I even find joy in that, as it gives me an opportunity to prove to my client how competent we are in overcoming challenges in order to serve them. Ah, yes, joy.

I have been running since I was nine years old. I run consistently because it brings me back to that childhood feeling of absolute freedom and sense of pure joy. I love the feeling of the outside air on my face. I like my Vermont view as I run through our Green Mountains. I like the solitude and sense of accomplishment my running brings me. Running is my joy, and it gives me the space I need to live a conscious life. I encourage people to find an activity that will bring them joy on a daily basis.

Ultimately, your joy will fuel your success.

Take Action – *Identify what brings you joy. It doesn't have to be physical. It can be anything that you do for you that will make you happy and bring joy to your life on a daily basis.*

"Just as your car runs more smoothly and requires less energy to go faster and farther when the wheels are in perfect alignment, you perform better when your thoughts, feelings, emotions, goals, and values are in balance."
—Brian Tracy

KINETIC ENERGY

THE **KINETIC ENERGY** OF an object is the energy it possesses due to its motion. It's defined as the work needed to accelerate a body of a given mass from rest to its stated velocity.

Life is fast, and as the years ebb and flow, I always notice that the more I have on my plate, the more I get done. You would really have to hunt to find a person that this does not apply to. This, my friends, is a form of kinetic energy. It's the result of energy that is produced from our very motion.

We all have *potential* to create great energy to move us towards our success, but until we put our thoughts into action, we have not realized any meaningful production.

Success is contingent on motion!

We all have opportunities presented to us, or ideas that strike us, and that creates potential. But unless we take action, we can't realize success. How do we harness our energy, take action and let it catapult us towards our personal and professional success, and realize our true potential?

Successful people harness their energy and take action.

In order to be successful you must be willing to take risks. And, once again, we encounter fear. Most people want a guarantee in life, and so they are fearful of an unknown outcome. When working with a client if I say that I "guarantee" that if they institute a new marketing program that they will succeed they are immediately on board. If I say, "Let's try this, analyze the results and then take next steps", the fear elevates and they hesitate. Where there is risk, there is fear and this is what holds people back from harnessing their energy and launching into action.

How do we capitalize on our kinetic energy?

- **Successful people are ready to move forward without a guarantee of success.** They understand that as they move forward there will be a need for course corrections along the way. They accept that the path from start to success is not linear.

- **Successful people are astute in evaluating results.** As they move forward they are open and welcome new opportunities. When progressing into new territory there will be unplanned challenges and corresponding detours. They are not afraid to investigate detours and understand that the unknown may lead to ventures that may be more in line with their goals.

- **Successful people move quickly and are willing to take on risk.** The Law of Probability states that the more you do, the more probable you will come upon what you are searching for. Some people call this luck. I believe that luck is the product of design.

- **Successful people utilize their energies to prepare.** People who are prepared inevitably come upon the opportunity necessary to succeed. This takes faith to prepare for the unknown and for those that do the appropriate preparation, their effort is rarely wasted.

How many times have you succumbed to the "what ifs" that come into your head? Every time you pander to fearful thoughts, you remain inert and unproductive and success will forever remain out of reach. I have over the years heard every excuse why someone is unable to go forward. For example, " I hate my job, my commute is lousy, I never see my family, and I don't have the time to look for a new job". I hear some rendition of this often. If you are unwilling to create space and take action, there will never be a better opportunity. If you leap-and, yes, I tell people to quit their job in order to open up space for something more positive to come in, you will be presented with a better opportunity. I know what you are thinking, "I can't", "What about the insurance?", "The economy is bad." Yes I know; but if you keep yourself in a vacuum of negativity there you will remain. When I left my career in Los Angeles for a life in Vermont, I did not have a job and truthfully the job I had in L.A. did not exist here in Vermont. It was an absolute leap of faith that if I put myself in the environment I wanted to be in opportunity would present and present it did. I never regretted my move or even second-guessed it. I have created amazing opportunities that would have never been present to me in my old harried life. Many clients have told me a little bravery teamed with energy and action changed their lives in outstanding ways.

Success will belong to the individuals that are willing to apply their energy to accept the risks and take action

Take Action – Identify what is holding you back from embracing your energy and taking action every day?

"Leaders don't create followers, they create more leaders."
—Tom Peters

A-Z Blueprint for Success

LEADERSHIP

OUR SUCCESS IN OUR personal and professional lives hinges on our ability to be effective leaders in our businesses, with our communities and for our families. *Leadership is about connecting emotionally with the people your life touches in order to inspire, motivate, teach, and guide them to achieve their true potential.*

Leadership simply is the ability to influence people. **An effective leader is able to lead a team towards success because he or she has a clear vision of the goal, is passionate for a cause, and is able to cultivate a culture of team growth.**

Here are a few tips on how to improve your leadership skills in order to create sustained success with your team members:

- **Leadership is about identifying and attracting productive team members and then developing them accordingly.**

  Assess the candidate's values and evaluate whether their value system resonates with yours. It is imperative that you **identify prospective candidates for your team who have the same high standards and value systems** as you do.

An effective leader can then nurture each individual's potential towards realized results. In addition, your performance will dictate how your team will perform. Be the positive example.

- **Leaders are relentless in pursuit of their goals and encourage their team members to take risks.**
  A leader perpetuates the belief in the organization or cause, which motivates the team to produce. Leaders are consistent in their efforts to move the team forward.

- **Leaders are skilled listeners.**
  Leaders listen and create effective communication processes to guide their team members individually to perform at their highest level. Leaders honor sharing of information and acknowledge that positive reinforcement motivates performance.

- **Leaders consistently apply good habits and use their time productively.**
  Leaders do not confuse activity for achievement. Mindless activity is not productive, and great leaders are able to teach this skill effectively to their team.

- **Leaders teach that we cannot control all of the challenges presented, but we can control our**

reactions. A leader recognizes that **rejection and other challenges are opportunities.**

Take Action – *Leadership is a refined skill and I encourage you to practice a bit of self-introspection to evaluate your leadership strengths and weaknesses. Improvement can only begin with recognition of your weak areas.*

"Mentoring is a brain to pick, an ear to listen, and a push in the right direction."

—John Crosby

MENTOR

I GREW UP IN an old-fashioned, big Catholic family. My siblings and I were born close together, with four of us born within four years, and then two additional brothers thrown into the mix thereafter. Six in all, with three girls and three boys. As you can imagine, it was a busy household. I was naturally first introduced to the benefits of mentorship through my siblings. I am the youngest girl and number four in the crew, so I was at the bottom of the barrel and relied heavily on my older brothers and sisters for guidance. To this day, my siblings are still my go-to people.

As I've moved through life, I have had many mentors along the way who have guided me, and I attribute my success to having had the benefit of mentors. I have had personal mentors who have aided me in showing the path to living a healthy productive life. I have also had professional mentors along the way, such as the partner at Coopers & Lybrand who guided me toward my professional focus when I was a CPA. A mentor shares his or her knowledge and helps pave the path for others who are coming up through the ranks. **The most significant benefit of having a mentor is the ability to save time. Time is our most valuable asset. Why waste it fumbling for answers when someone with more experience and wisdom can interpret the myriad paths and**

information that needs to be processed? The guidance a mentor provides is invaluable.

The benefit of this relationship is not, however, one-sided. In fact, it is mutually beneficial. A mentor is afforded the opportunity to improve his or her leadership skills and the satisfaction of helping someone move closer to success. I like mentoring younger people, as it creates a link to that generation, giving me a view into their perspective and their ideas. Plus they always introduce me to some new technology!

How do we develop an effective and mutually beneficial mentorship relationship?

- **Identify an individual in your industry who has excelled and exhibits a similar value system, is trustworthy, and willing to share their knowledge.** This person should inspire you towards achievement. He or she will be a skilled listener, offer direction, and be particularly astute in interpreting your challenges. Approach the individual with clarity as to what you're expecting from the relationship. Communicate the information or specific skills you would like assistance in developing. Ultimately, surround yourself with positive people that you admire.

- **Be cognizant that this relationship, although mutually beneficial, is most likely more to your favor.** So in light of that fact, *be exceedingly clear with expectations and extremely respectful of a mentor's*

A-Z Blueprint for Success

time. Formulate what will work for both of you. I have actually asked someone to speak to me every Friday for 10 minutes in order to get a response to two questions. This individual was in high demand and I wanted to be enormously respectful of her time. My efficiency ultimately paid off for me, and I'm sure benefited my mentor, if only in that it made them feel good to know they were helpful in guiding me to the next level.

- **It is up to you to get the most out of the relationship.** *Be clear in your questions, be gracious in receiving criticism, do the work as best you can, and learn from your mistakes.* A successful mentorship requires a desire to succeed, and a bit of courage on your part to be honest with yourself and your mentor about your shortcomings. In the end, it is worth the effort.

I do hope that you can experience a productive, positive relationship from both the mentor and student perspectives, as it is enormously beneficial. Life is short, so if you can create positive alliances that aid you in getting closer to your goals quicker, then do it!

> ***Take Action** – Find a mentor and be a mentee!*

"The successful networkers I know, the ones receiving tons of referrals and feeling truly happy about themselves, continually put the other person's needs ahead of their own."
—Bob Burg

A-Z Blueprint for Success

NETWORKING

NETWORKING CULTIVATES LONG LASTING relationships. Let's face it-every successful business is based on relationships. We all network every day informally. When you're at the vet and you bump into an acquaintance, you inevitably begin to talk about business. We also network online through social media channels.

There are the more formal avenues of networking when you attend an organized event that brings together a group of people with a common association. At these formal events, you often witness a few classic networking blunders. Someone approaches you and within 0.5 seconds is handing you his business card and launching into a sales pitch as your eyes glaze over and you desperately search for a way out of the conversation.

Networking is the skill of building mutually beneficial relationships. Let's talk about a few DOs and DON'Ts to ensure your networking (whether formal, informal or online) is effective:

- **Your attitude when networking has an enormous impact on your result.**
  Though your initial goal may be a bit selfish, try to go into a networking situation with the thought

of wanting to help someone else. Be genuinely interested in reaching out for the sole purpose of discovering more about someone else. If you go into a relationship with the idea of bringing value with no expectation of return, then you lend credibility to who you are and what you represent. Don't go into a networking opportunity shortsighted with only a self-serving goal in mind.

- **Use discretion when building a network**
  There is a common saying our grandmother's preached, "Be careful of the company you keep." There is only so much time, so whom we choose to connect with will have great impact on our success. Be insightful and cultivate contacts that are meaningful and valid. Don't build a network without any forethought of validity of the relationships you pursue.

- **Be consistent in your efforts to network.**
  It takes time to build a network, and there are many networking avenues to choose from. Online social networking through Facebook, LinkedIn, and online public forums are great and give you a vast reach at your fingertips. You may also choose to build a network more traditionally, like attending organized association meetings or conferences.

I have a friend, who is a marketing guru, and she abhors the formalized association gatherings, so she prefers to network online. I like meeting people face-to-face and am comfortable with a speaking engagement and the post-interaction with the audience. I also enjoy the networking through technology. The trick is to know what forum is most comfortable for you. If you are comfortable with online networking, be mindful. Online blunders are just as common as in-person blunders! Your behavior will be noted and seen by all, so remember to display the same etiquette you would in person, because there is a "real" person on the other side. Whatever route you take, and I encourage you to try all of them, make sure you are comfortable. Be consistent, and you will see positive results.

> ***Take Action*** *– Find a Network where you can serve others and it will serve you.*

"Once you have a clear picture of your priorities-that is values, goals, and high leverage activities-organize around them." **-Stephen Covey**

ORGANIZATION

"I can't find it"
"I have no idea what my biggest priority is today"
"I don't know what my breakeven point is in my business"

HOW MANY OF YOU have made one of these statements today? The ability to organize your work area, your agenda and your finances is pivotal to working effectively and efficiently. If you are disorganized and harried in your efforts to complete the day's tasks, time and efficiency is lost and the quality of your work will suffer.

A common thread among successful people is their ability to organize every aspect of their lives. The ability to organize properly increases your productivity. Maintaining organization is a challenge, as we try to stay focused on our goals while juggling the myriad of responsibilities pulling at our time. We need to manage many obligations beyond our professional lives, and the key to maintaining the necessary balance is organization! Organization allows us to keep our productivity level as high as possible.

Here are a few tips to help you get organized, and more importantly, stay organized:

- **Achieve financial organization:**
  I recommend QuickBooks for business and Quicken for personal finance. These are very user-friendly programs, and they will keep you financially on track. I am a huge fan of being clear as to what your income and expenses are on a daily, weekly, monthly and annual basis.

- **Stay on task:**
  I recommend Google Docs and Google Calendar for keeping you on task. You can access these from any computer or PDA. Plan ahead each day to stay on task as you move through your day. I guarantee that you will get more accomplished in a day if you plan it. I have an iPhone, Macbook and iPad as tools to keep me on task. You don't need all of these, but find what works for you. A pad and paper with copious notes can do the job for some.

- **Use the *Touch-It-Once-Rule:***
  This rule will help you get organized, rid you of the clutter, and increase your efficiency. As you move through the day, touch each piece of paper just once. This rule helps me to stay focused while I'm working. I touch or read a document once and then file it appropriately. Whether you are filing for future reference, or putting a document in, its final holding place, only deal with it once.

These are the three tips that will have the greatest impact on keeping you organized. If you are completely disorganized and have absolutely no capacity to do it yourself, I recommend hiring a person to come in and get you set up. Whatever a professional charges to come in to organize your office, your home, and your financial systems, the fee will pay for itself in increased productivity. I guarantee it!

Take Action – *Organize where you live and where you work, and don't forget to organize your finances!*

"Ambition is the path to success; persistence is the vehicle you arrive in."
—William Eardley IV

PERSISTENCE

Persistence is crucial to your success. It is a quality that can be developed and is a necessary habit in order to avoid failure.

THERE IS NO MORE important component to success than persistence. Nothing can replace persistence; neither talent nor intelligence. You can be the smartest most talented person in your profession and fail because you are unable to persist through adversity. The ability to continue steadfastly in pursuit of your dreams and goals in the face of challenge is the deciding factor between success and failure. Persistence connects the dots in our plans.

Often people are so very close to success, but they lack the persistence to get through that last hurdle that would have gotten them to the summit. Franklin D. Roosevelt said, "When you come to the end of your rope, tie a knot and hold on." Persistence is both the desire and the choice to refuse failure. Persistence is the refusal to let fear get the best of you. Persistence can taste so bitter yet the results so very sweet.

Whether I am coaching a client or mothering my girls I find myself going back to the principal of persistence as the great resource to attain my goals. Is persistence a skill that can be learned? It is a skill that can be learned, sharpened and nurtured. Yes!

Persistence is a result of the following five key components. If you address each of these areas, the power of persistence will catapult you towards your desired result:

- **Passion**:
  If you are passionate with an intense desire to succeed in your pursuit, persistence comes naturally. Whatever the dream you pursue, you must be exceedingly passionate in order to tough out the low spots. Passion is the ultimate driving force behind persistence.

Unfortunately, just because you are passionate about a particular project does not necessarily mean that it should become a business. Oh, so many times, people fail spectacularly because the only supporting block in their business is their passion for the cause, the product or the service. Passion alone will not equate to business success. So before you decide to take Aunt Bee's chicken potpie recipe global, be sure the business plan has more than just passion behind it!

- **Clarity**:
  If you have a clearly defined goal and strategy behind what you want, persistence will follow your motivation. Your clarity about your goal is and your recognition of the positive outcome will create persistence. Whatever your goal is get a

picture of it in your head, use it as a screen saver on your computer, or create a vision board.

Your supporting strategy of your goals should include all potential obstacles you may encounter. Many of the toughest obstacles are unforeseen; however, by preparing for possible obstructions you gain the clarity and guidance you need to persist uphill when you need to.

- **Belief**:
  If you believe in your ability to accomplish your dream, you will be persistent. The most important person who needs to believe in your dream is you. You alone must believe more than anyone else in the world. There are a million examples of success stories where the only person who believed in the project was the person creating it. I recommend the book, Ignore Everybody by Hugh MacLeod. Hugh MacLeod speaks volumes on creativity and forging ahead in our risk-averse world and the importance of believing in your own creativity.

- **Organization**:
  If you have a carefully laid-out strategy, it is easy to persist in accomplishing each expectation. Having a well-organized plan is key to persisting through the very messy process of success. It is so easy for our attention to become diverted by disorganization and then we lose our persistence because we don't know where we are going. A well thought out, step-by-step organized plan

will aid you in being persistent because you are accomplishing your plan in bite sized chunks.

- **Support**:
  If you surround yourself with supportive and positive people, you will be more likely to persist in your pursuit. Period. Having a great support team is crucial to your ability to persist. Edit as necessary. If you have a negative influence in your life it is important to protect yourself and your dream-remove them. Removing negativity creates the necessary space for the positive, which always appears when it is invited and there is room.

Take Action – If you are lacking in persistence, evaluate yourself based on the above, find your weakness and create a plan of persistence.

"There is more difference in the quality of our pleasures than in the amount."
—Ralph Waldo Emerson

QUALITY

WE ARE A QUANTITY-DRIVEN society, from our massive consumerism to our need to amass an abundance of Facebook friends. This scenario plays out in both our professional and our personal lives. In order to be successful, we must pay attention to the quality of our relationships.

When I started my marketing business many moons ago, I would accept anyone who came knocking at my door. In my zeal to succeed at my business, I needed to gain clients. So, I would work with anyone who appeared. I was, to say the least, not very discriminating, and I paid for that by having a few clients with whom the margins were small and the effort to keep them as clients was huge.

Over time, I learned that all clients are not created equal, and the quality of my clients was more important to my business success than the quantity of clients. The same holds true, of course, in our personal lives. The quality of the people with whom we surround ourselves is much more important than the quantity.

We cost ourselves time when we select less-than-ideal clients, team members, and friends, trying to develop relationships that are neither beneficial nor necessary to growing our business or enriching our lives. Time really is money.

Well, since time is our most valuable asset, and if we are wasting our time on non-productive relationships, then we are also throwing our money out the door. This can be a very real obstacle to success!

How do we qualify our potential clients or team members in order to ensure quality?

Here are a few tips:

- **Build a list of values and qualities important to you.**
  Rank order them from most important to least important. Understand qualities that are deal breakers. This will help you create a profile of what you deem a quality potential prospect. For example, I highly value honesty, trust, intelligence, and I absolutely abhor lack of work ethic. As a result, a lazy person is a deal breaker for me, and I won't work with that person, even if he or she is honest, trustworthy and smart. Whether you are hiring an employee, pursuing a new client or developing a friendship your values must be in alignment.

- **Create relationships that are mutually beneficial and balanced.**
  Each party in the relationship needs to give and receive equally. To assess whether a potential client or team member is viable, you must ask open-ended questions (who, what, why, when) in order to have a clear understanding of that person's

needs. Once you fully understand his or her needs, you can then understand whether your solution will meet those needs and wants, and decide if there is potential for a quality relationship.

Here are a few examples of open-ended questions to qualify a potential client:

Who: Who is the decision maker? Is this the person who gives the final yes on the deal? If not, you are wasting your time and effort. When you are presenting a new product or opportunity, it is a waste of time and effort if you are not presenting to the person who gives the final YES.

What: What is the expectation that this person has regarding your product or opportunity?

Why: Why would he or she be interested in your product or opportunity? What solution are you providing to that person's needs or desires?

When: When do you anticipate taking action? This will guide you on their timetable.

In the end, if you consistently qualify people in your life, you will choose quality clients, team members and friends, and you will be more successful in your endeavors.

> **Take Action –** *Create a list of qualifying questions as a strategy to help you focus on establishing quality relationships.*

*"Surround yourself with only people who
are going to lift you higher."*
—Oprah Winfrey

RELATIONSHIPS

I HAVE HAD MANY clients who will report that a particular relationship is creating an obstacle in achieving their goals. Unfortunately, it takes just a few negative people in your inner circle who are not supportive to create a block. If you have a new business that you are working hard to develop, and a few key people giving negative messages, it makes your pursuit to success much harder. They have a tendency to reinforce your fears. When we encounter negativity, it is hard to go forward, especially if the negativity comes from our circle of influence. One of the most powerful, deciding factors of our success is the people with whom we choose to interact.

If you look at the quality and success of your five closest friends and colleagues, you will probably find that all of you have aspired and reached the same level.

If we surround ourselves with people who are successful, energetic, positive, creative and inspiring, they will motivate and influence us to be at that level. If we associate with negative, unhappy people who are operating below their potential, then we will settle at the low end of success and limit our own achievement, too.

Here are a few relationship strategies to help you develop positive associations and respond to negativity that is out of your control:

Pay attention to the people in your life and how you feel after you have been with them. If you feel energized by their presence, they're keepers. If you feel drained after having spent time with them, then edit them out. The people we work with and socialize with have tremendous impact. Seek out positive influencers.

Notice I used the phrase "choose to interact with". We choose the quality of people we associate with in most instances, and we have the power to nourish or cut off our relationships. So if you are surrounding yourself with people you do not want to be like, then it's time to edit them out of your life and seek out people who will be supportive of your goals. We need people we admire and trust in our lives.

When you edit your relationships, you'll **make room for positive people to come in.** If you are having trouble finding positive connections, don't worry. Read positive books, magazines, listen to tapes with positive messages, and soon you will be attracting people who also subscribe to the positive theory.

How do you react to those negative people we can't easily edit and delete? What do you do when you have a negative team member you must work with? Or what do you do when you have a family member who draws on your energy? In these situations when you must spend time with the negative people, you must control your thoughts. ***Harness your own*** *thought process* **and hang on tight to your beliefs,** and don't let their negative commentary in. Just smile, nod, and move on.

> **Take Action** – *Evaluate your relationships and edit, as needed even when this proves difficult.*

"Don't aim for success if you want it; just do what you love and believe in, and it will come naturally."
—David Frost

SUCCESS

WHAT IS SUCCESS? HOW do we know that we've been successful? After I teach a class on business development, leadership, goal strategy-whatever the subject-I always give the participants an evaluation form. I want to know how my information is received, whether I'm clear in my presentation, and if they feel they can take the information and immediately integrate it into their lives in a positive fashion. Heck, I even want to know if the room is too cold, or if I am speaking too fast!

I am really looking for honest feedback; since it is the only way I can know where I need to improve my presentations. This week, however, I jokingly said to someone, "Please send the evaluation form so that I can know whether I am a success or not!"

It is natural to look for external cues to evaluate our performance. However, the true answer as to whether you are a success or not lies within.

Success requires a balancing act of your professional and personal life and requires continuous attention and action on the details. A few considerations when creating a life of success:

1. Strive to be successful on a daily basis. Action oriented people win.
2. Create a clear vision of your life of success and keep that vision front and center on a daily basis.
3. Understand and honor your core values. All action should serve your core values.
4. Develop and sustain healthy habits.
5. Be decisive and do not procrastinate. Do not fall into the fear trap that will keep you inert.
6. Realize that all success comes with a price. Success requires hard work and there are sacrifices.
7. Believe in yourself even when nobody else will.
8. Define your goal and supporting strategy so that you have a clear direction.
9. Dedicate yourself to ultimately serving others in all that you do.
10. FOCUS

Personally I feel that Success is simply knowing that I have given 100% of my ability on a daily basis to my family, my business and myself. At the end of the day, I want to know I did the best I could with every situation that was presented. Success is the direct result of effort, and if you are giving 100% of your effort every day, then you are successful. You, and only you, can establish whether you have given 100% or not.

How do we keep ourselves on target while moving towards our success?

Yes, I have to bring up goals again. I feel that my family will have "Goal Setter" carved on my headstone! Again, success cannot be achieved without a clearly thought out set of goals and strategies to support your dreams.

Your goals should be continuously reviewed and revised. Meeting your goals inch by inch will get you to your personal and professional success.

It is also important to recognize and reward yourself for your achievements. Truly every goal must have an associated reward. How else will you know you succeeded? Set a reward and don't overlook it and be sure you do reward yourself along the way. It is so easy to just keep going forward and hurry through one goal after another. Enjoy your successes, and you will be energized for the next step.

Also, be gentle on yourself as you analyze your failures. ***Missteps are just opportunities to move you closer to your success.***

> **Take Action** – *Write down your definition of personal and professional success and a corresponding reward as you attain each goal.*

"Time has more value than money. You can get more money, but you cannot get more time."
—Jim Rohn

TIME

WHEN I LIVED IN Los Angeles and worked as a CPA in a high-rise building surrounded by smog and a stressed environment, I spent hours every day fighting traffic to get to my office, worked very long days, went home and returned again the next day, like a faithful soldier, to repeat the madness. In a nutshell, my life consisted of traffic, work, sleep, and it was completely void of any personal enjoyment. *I was trading all of my time for money.*

Eventually as I got older, and my husband and I wanted to start a family, I wasn't willing to trade my time for money anymore. I also wasn't willing to live in a crowded city with smog, earthquakes, and a heavy dose of crime.

Our solution was to move to beautiful, safe, friendly Vermont! Jumping out of the corporate whirlwind and landing in Vermont was the best decision I ever made. I have learned to live a much more balanced life and I no longer trade all of my time for money.

My business has a nationwide presence, thanks to the Internet, so my professional life is intact in this rural environment. I decide when I work, when I play, and how much money I make. I dictate the terms of my life, not some corporation. My life is now flexible, so if the kids have a snow day from school, I go skiing with them.

I don't think you need to move to a rural environment to avoid trading your time for money; that solution may be too drastic for some people. I just don't believe you have to choose between money or time wherever you live.

Here are a few steps you can take to help you reclaim your time and allow yourself to live a balanced yet profitable life:

- **Figure out your four areas of focus in your life.** What is most important to you? **Once you have identified where your focus should be, then all of your time, attention and money should go to these four areas.** And, again, if you want to know your current focus, take a look at your checkbook! How we spend our money tells us our values and where we spend our time. If you look at my checkbook, you will see my money goes to my family (food, skis, books), my health (gym membership), my business (more books) and my community (donations).

- **Leverage every timesaving tool available to maximize the time you spend on your business.** I automate everything I can from lead generation to qualifying, and I only spend time in areas of my business requiring my direct attention. Automation allows my business to produce income while I am off skiing.

- **Create a financial strategy that provides a residual stream of passive income.**

  Passive income can be generated by investing, for example, or by owning real estate and collecting rent. A few other passive income generating options would be network marketing or earning royalties from the hit song you've written! *The goal is to create a stream of residual income, so that you earn the money you need to support the life you desire without trading all of your time.*

There are many paths to producing residual income, and I encourage you to find the right opportunity for yourself. Look for a system that can be easily duplicated to continuously produce income, and then you will have more of what matters in life — time.

At the end of life, people never wish they made more money, but they always wish for more time with the people they love. Relationships and experiences create the rich fabric of our lives, so finding a way to make money without trading our precious time is a worthy goal.

All of us struggle to utilize our time more efficiently. We all wish for more than our 24 hours and often we attempt to expand our day by sleeping less. I employ this tactic often, but it is certainly not a long-term solution. Here are a few suggestions to help you get more productivity out of your day:

- **Turn the television off.**

  Here is a shocking statistic; according to the A.C. Nielsen Co., the average American watches 9 years of television by the time they reach 65. Nine years! Open a book or your tablet and read to stretch your knowledge and entertain. If you are truly inclined to watch a favorite show, use a DVR so that you can whip through those commercials.

- **Watch the clock as you surf the web and imbibe social media.**
  We all need to be in touch and it is a great connector for business and personal use; however, watch the clock and don't waste time on senseless browsing. Also, check your email at set times throughout the day. Incessant connection is an enormous distraction.

- **Hire people to do work that is not necessary for you to do.**
  Your talent needs to be free for more important productive tasks. Pay someone clean your home, detail your car, paint the house, file reports etc. My rule is that if I can pay someone $100.00 or less to do it, I pay. Paying someone else to do tasks that are not part of your focus will allow you to earn more and protect your time.

- **Schedule your day every day to help you stay focused.**
  Every night, plan your next day. Write it down and check the items off your list as you progress through your day. You will find yourself more focused and less apt to give in to distractions.

- **Multi-task through mundane parts of your day.** Listen to a book on tape while commuting to increase your knowledge or relax and create enjoyable downtime while the freeway hijacks you.

If you are not sure where you are wasting your precious time keep a log. At the end of the week I promise that your least productive areas will be apparent.

Take Action – *Identify how you utilize your time and create a strategy to increase productivity and protect your biggest but most limited resource – time.*

"Trusting your individual uniqueness challenges you to lay yourself open."
—James Broughton

A-Z Blueprint for Success

UNIQUE

IT IS CRUCIAL TO be unique in this crazy, competitive world. The facts are that **we all have the same access to the same marketing channels that reach the same audiences.**

So how do you succeed when it seems we are all marginalized by "equal opportunities"? Well, the answer is to be unique and don't just flow with what you think is expected. Go for the unexpected and embrace your own uniqueness. In the end, your unique qualities or talents will differentiate you from the rest of the crowd.

Recently, I received an email from a gal who participated in one of my classes on business development. In the class, we discussed how to develop a business by leveraging the Internet as well as implementing traditional marketing methods. Well, this woman, whom I'll call Zany, emailed to tell me how great the new capture page on her website was working for her. A prospect came through her capture page and began a discussion with Zany about joining her business.

This person told Zany that she had previously been approached by someone else presenting the same opportunity, but she was not impressed enough to pursue it. Now, however, she wanted to investigate again because

Zany's marketing style and presentation attracted her, and she felt Zany was someone she could trust.

Now, let's be clear, the capture page (which is a landing page that collects visitors' information) was attractive to this person because of what Zany had written. Zany writes with a unique style, and it separates her from "the pack." Ultimately, it is our uniqueness that pulls people in.

People or organizations are always telling us how to be, what to say, and how to act in order to be successful using their definitions. But success comes from embracing our own unique qualities, characteristics, thought processes, and presentation. When we present in a way that truly represents our own creative genius, as Zany did, our chances of success skyrockets.

If you want to be really successful, don't follow the crowd. Be unique and trust your own instincts. Today, we have so many terrific avenues to present our business opportunities, and if we are clever in presenting, we will stand out from the crowd.

Again, I recommend, Hugh MacLeod's *Ignore Everybody*. This book will inspire you to embrace your own unique capacity for creativity.

"The pain of making the necessary sacrifices always hurts more than you think it's going to. I know. It sucks. That being said, doing something seriously creative is one of the most amazing experiences one can have, in this or any other lifetime. If you can pull it off, it's worth it. Even if you don't end up pulling it off, you'll learn many incredible, magical, valuable things. It's NOT doing it when you know full well

you HAD the opportunity - that hurts FAR more than any
failure."

—**Hugh MacLeod**, *How To Be Creative*

> **Take Action** – Be courageous and don't shy
> away from what makes you unique.

"Share our similarities, celebrate our differences."
—M. Scott Peck

A-Z Blueprint for Success

VALUE PROPOSITION

MANY YEARS AGO WHEN I changed my life and jumped off of the corporate treadmill in Los Angeles for a quiet life in Vermont, I started a marketing company that provided advertising premiums. This industry is a highly commoditized industry, meaning that my business was providing a product that almost any other vendor could supply. Therefore, the industry as a whole was enormously based on price competition.

I knew that because of this characteristic within the industry, I had to identify and market based on a clear value proposition that would separate my business from my competition very clearly. My value proposition was that my business would provide creative solutions to our clients' marketing challenges with unique products and strategies. I marketed our services according to our unique capabilities and built a million dollar business based on this value proposition.

Almost every new business is started based on the belief that the business will provide something of unique value that is not currently being provided by the competition.

Having a clear definition of what is unique about you and your business, so that you market based on your own unique **value proposition is vital in order to obtain results.**

Your value proposition is the answer to why a person should do business with you.

What value do you bring that will entice people to not only take notice, but take action and choose you, your business, or your team over the competition?

The first step prior to launching your business is to identify your value proposition. This step is not to be taken lightly and takes a great deal of time and effort. In the end understanding and promoting your business based on your value proposition will mean the difference between success and failure.

- **Identify your Value Proposition.**
  Reflect upon your business, your product, your service to clearly identify what is unique about what you offer. Know who your competition is, and what you offer that overrides the competition. Understand the choices your potential customers have and what you will deliver to provide a solution and motivate those customers to do business with you. What benefit do you provide that your competition does not? Do an analysis to clearly understand why a prospect needs to buy from you.

Clearly understand who your target market is, what its primary concerns or needs are, and why your opportunity is the best solution for that group of people. If you have been in business for a period of time and are not sure what it is that separates you personally from the crowd, go to a few of your existing clients and interview them to find out why they chose you or your opportunity over your competition. Ask them:

"What is the most important value that we are fulfilling for you?" "Why do you choose our product?"

- **Articulate your Value Proposition.**

  Once you have identified what makes your business truly unique, you must articulate it clearly through every marketing channel you choose to utilize. As I have previously discussed, the amount of time we have to get our point across to our prospects is very short, so your value proposition must be concise, clear and succinct so it is easily communicated to your customers. Tell your customers what you deliver that your competitors do not.

An example of a value proposition statement: **XYZ Corporation is the exclusive dealer of the high efficiency ABC lathe tooling. Our customers have experienced increased production levels by as much as 50%, which translates into substantial increased revenue.**

This is an effective proposition because it states that they have a unique position over their competition -"Exclusive dealer" and the statement quantifies the success experienced by their customers - "50% increased productivity".

> ***Take Action*** *– Create a powerful value proposition for your business. Analyze it, identify it, write it down and create a marketing position to support it.*

"Nothing will work unless you do." **- John Wooden**

A-Z Blueprint for Success

WORK ETHIC

UNLESS YOU WIN THE lottery, success will come with a price tag and that price tag is work. There is absolutely no substitute for a work ethic. Success will not be thrown at your door without a good old fashion dose of hard work.

The goal you are pursuing will not magically appear. My daughter Carling is 14. She is a great kid and in every way what I had hoped for. She is acutely aware of who she is and quietly confident. She loves her family and prefers us to her friends. (Yes, I know I am on borrowed time with this) She loves her 10-year-old sister. She is a skier, runner, and tennis player. She is an accomplished pianist and a fine writer. She is sweet and compassionate. She has friends here at home and in China, and she adores Taylor Swift. She works hard and is an achiever, and I am very proud of her. She lives a very fortunate and privileged life here in Vermont. Now the reason I am telling you about this delightful child is that we were speaking once again about the prospect of her getting a summer job, to which she retorted "Mom, only the poor kids have jobs at the age of 14"! Well, I asked her about her assets and how her investments were doing and quietly reminded her that:

SHE IS A POOR KID!

I do not want to introduce yet another entitled young adult into our work force.

Work ethic is king.

I was a teenager in the 70's, and we were a big Catholic family with 6 kids. This was truly the norm back then - lots of kids and a strong work ethic were highly valued traits. If you wanted anything extra beyond food and shelter, such as a pet rock or mood ring or perhaps a new pair of bellbottoms, you worked for it! There were no handouts. Well, when I was 11 I got a paper route. Best job in the world, and what did I learn from that paper route?

- **Entrepreneurship:**
  That paper route was truly my first step in developing my business acumen. I learned how to run my little mini paper enterprise so that I could maximize my cash flow in an effort to support my mood ring habit. I learned quickly that the more customers I got the more money I made. This was also a 7-day paper, so if I needed to take time off, I had to train someone to step into my position and carry those papers to my customers as if they were gold. Yes, this was my first experience of running a business, and experience is a great teacher.

- **Motivation:**
  From time to time the paper I slugged around-*The Post Star* - would hold a contest and give a prize for the person who acquired the most customers within a specific period of time. Oh, boy, I would knock on every door I passed on my route who was not receiving the paper and tell them the great benefits of receiving *The Post Star,* morning paper.

Of course, I would tell them how dependable I was. I learned how to sell and present the benefits of my product and tout the guarantee of great customer service.

- **Early Bird Gets the Worm**:
  I still live by this. That paper route taught me to get up early and begin my day productively. I would get up at 4:00 in the morning so my customers would have their paper by the time they were reaching for their 6:00 coffee. My mom actually insisted that was what the world needed – a newspaper by 6:00! I can still remember the quiet of the morning with the snow squeaking under my boots and the cold air in my lungs. It would be dark and the stars would be shining, and there I was, walking through my quiet town delivering the paper! I still love to get up early in the morning and jumpstart my day.

- **Quality Control**:
  Oh, yes. I wanted my tips, and I learned quickly who liked their paper between their doors and, if it was raining or snowing, I was sure to walk up to every door and make sure that paper was safely tucked in between the doors to keep it dry. We didn't have plastic bags back then and unless you wanted to diminish your tips, you made sure that paper stayed dry!

- **Customer Service**:
  Delivery on time, every time. If you noticed the papers piling up, you realized they had gone on vacation and had forgotten to call the paper

office to hold the papers. So you took the papers home with you and delivered all of them to your customer when you saw the lights were back on in the house, and you did it with a smile. Now, I was a kid so there were some screw-ups. For instance, I did walk up to the door to keep the paper dry when necessary, but on dry mornings I liked to fold it really tight and whip it at their front door. Remember the old aluminum doors? Well, if you hit that baby just right, the noise was just superb, and you were sure to let your customer know just how early you had arrived! Not nice and, yes, I learned that probably was not the best customer service.

- **Money:**
  This was my first experience with money. I learned quickly you needed to account for all of those pennies, give up what the paper deserved and, if you wanted more money, you needed to get more customers. I learned that if you could get people to pay early, the paper would give you a percentage of the early payment. My first experience with 2% 10 net 30.

- **Balance:**
  I held on to this paper route until I was 16 and could get a job at our local tennis and racquetball club. During those years with the paper route I learned that I needed to juggle school and working in the early morning in addition to my music lessons and sports practices. I learned that I needed to get my homework done quickly so that I could get to bed at a decent hour. I learned to juggle

my responsibilities and this alone has served me well.

- **Value of a job**:
  Back then kids wanted paper routes. They were coveted, and if you screwed up there was someone who was dying to replace you. Also, back in the "old days" if you screwed up, you got called out on it. Fired. Done. Kaput. There was no soft angle or concern for a kid's ego. If you didn't meet the expectation, you were fired. I learned to value my job, and I was sure to do it above and beyond the expectations of the paper company and my customer.

I feel very blessed that I was born into a poor family and learned the great value of hard work when I was young. I wish that my daughters can look forward to an experience of equal value. If it involves getting up before the crack of dawn and walking up hill with bags on their backs in the elements, all the better!

When we all look back at our first jobs I'm sure most would agree that our first job, like our first love, was our greatest teacher. All the experiences gained from that early morning paper route come into play every day as I move my businesses towards success, and hard work will forever remain my most valued trait.

> *Take Action* — *Reflect on your past experience and your present work ethic. Does it match up? How can you ramp up your efforts?*

"Your premium brand had better be delivering something special, or it's not going to get the business."
—Warren Buffett

A-Z Blueprint for Success

X FACTOR

SUCCESS IS DEPENDENT ON a person or business possessing a bit of an X factor. They have some quality that catapults them above the competition. The X factor is an attribute that allows one to have a positive influence. It is that special element that attracts people.

For example, when I was getting ready to move out of Los Angeles and rebuild my life, I visited several different states, such as Colorado and Oregon, before I settled on Vermont. Vermont had an X factor other areas didn't — beauty and close proximity to a few major cities like New York City and Boston. Vermont would allow me to live in a tranquil environment while having access to a city when I had a craving for the stimulation only a big city can offer.

When I look at hiring a new team member for my business, I am driven by the search to find the X factor in an individual. I am looking for what that individual offers that sets him or her apart from the rest of the contenders.

When I am consulting to help a business succeed, I am always looking for that business's X factor. What does that company offer that makes it stand out from the crowd? Once we have identified the company's X factor and developed a marketing plan around it, the chance of the business succeeding greatly increases.

If you think about your life, you will find that it revolves around X factors. Every business you frequent has an X factor that drives you there. Every person you choose to interact with has something special that attracts you.

The X factor in our life can be developed, and that is what will make us successful. So how do we develop our X factor? It is a process that is on par with brand development.

- **Understand the market niche that your product or service is fulfilling.**
  I mean, really do the research and find out who your competitors are. Find out what each competitor's X factor is.

- **Identify *your* X factor.**
  What need is your product or service fulfilling in the marketplace that differentiates you from the crowd? Go back to the chapter in this book on Value Proposition and get really clear what you are bringing to the marketplace that will set you apart.

- **Once you have developed your X factor, then it must be nurtured as time goes on.**
  Your X factor needs to be continuously fine-tuned as new competition comes into the market and various changes are introduced.

Take Action — Identify, develop and nurture your X factor.

"Youth has no age."
—Pablo Picasso

GEN Y

HOW MANY TIMES HAVE we heard someone exclaim, "I don't understand this younger generation!"? There is frustration when clients from differing generations clash. I have heard from many a client bewildered by a younger target audience. Approximately 80% of my clients in my ad specialty business are between the ages of 25 and 40. I will confirm for you that selling to the young demographic, or as they are known Gen Y, is a completely different ballgame than selling to the Gen X or Baby Boom generations. For those of us who have been in business for a long time, it can be a frustrating pursuit.

To be wildly successful, we must love thy customer. It is just one of those business golden rules. So, let me introduce you to your customer. I hope this introduction will lead to love and understanding!

These dates are not set in stone and what I'm going to discuss somewhat generalized, but it will help you to gain a better understanding of your target audiences.

Baby Boomer: (Born 1944-1964) My husband and I are boomers. We bookend this era with his birth in 1944 and mine in 1964. Yes, we are a May-December relationship, but that is another story. This was the Post WWII gen and they grew up in a very cohesive national culture. There were only three television channels, and they all were tuned in to the same messages. This group was a tad self-righteous and, thankfully, they expected the world -post war- to continue to improve. The boomers were responsible for expansion of freedoms. They fought for civil rights and the rights of women and are a bit idolized for their contributions to change. They contended with the Vietnam War, assassinations and enjoyed the success of our Nation's first walk on the moon.

Gen X (Born 1966 -1980) I'm really a Gen X gal. Gen X is sometimes referred to as the middle child. Sandwiched between the social change boomers and the techy Y generation, this group has no real identity. I remember quite clearly the recession in the 70s with parents out of work, the oil crisis with cars lined up for gas during the energy crisis. We had the Chernobyl disaster and watched the space shuttle Challenger blow up right before our eyes. Just as we graduated college in the mid 80s and got our first jobs, we experienced black Monday on 10/19/87. I was working for Coopers & Lybrand, and my apartment mate was laid off. Fortunately, I was always employed. This generation was marked with an uncertain future. Ah, the pain of being a middle child.

Gen Y (Born Roughly 1977-1995) This generation is profoundly adept with communications, media and digital technology. They are connected! Tech-savvy is the very definition of this group. They run their lives technically and prefer to communicate via text or email rather than face to face. This is a big challenge for us old school kids who still believe in relationship selling.

They watched their parents, the Gen X crew, work hard to support their families and obtain a higher standard of living than their post WWII folks, all the while sacrificing their family time and, in some cases, any resemblance of a quality of life. Their parents gave their lives to the corporate world and found out that the corporate world in return was not so loyal in the mergers and acquisition period of the 80s. The Gen Y group saw this and decided they were going to live their lives on their own terms, so they have high expectations of their employers and are more apt to leave a company for other horizons in pursuit of their definition of success. Corporate loyalty is not part of their playbook, and they have a better understanding of work/life balance than previous generations. How dare they want to live life first and work second? This can be perceived as the "narcissist or entitled" group, but they just believe in living life on their terms.

They are confident, achievement oriented, and their ambition is apparent. I believe we will see more entrepreneurs from this generation than any previous generation.

Gen Y is financially smart. These kids have watched financial melt downs since the first dot. com bubble burst in the early 90s, and they are very aware that they need to take control of their own financial future as much as possible.

So, watch out, these kids move. They are keen on developing skills and moving forward as quickly as possible. Change is not only embraced, but also expected. The challenge for corporations today is how do we retain Gen Y talent?

So the question my client posed was, "How do we reach this Gen Y demographic?"

This generation is going be part of our target market for a very long time, so here are a few pointers:

- **They run their lives technically.**

  They prefer to communicate via text or email rather than face to face (and truthfully they prefer text) So you are going to have to go beyond the belly-to-belly traditional relationship model and integrate every tech communication method possible if you intend to reach them.

- **They are very sophisticated.**

  They have had lots of exposure to "wow" which makes this generation pretty tough to impress! They have seen it all, so traditional marketing channels are not going to hit with them. You need to be as creative as possible to draw them in. Think guerilla marketing – it works!

- **Their attention span is short.**

  Thanks to the availability of information on the web--- and this generation in particular would like all information to be presented as quickly as a text-their attention span is miniscule. You need to be creative, clear and concise in your outreach. Be brief, engaging and memorable.

- **They will not look for you.**

  You have to find them, and the best place is on social network sites: Facebook, LinkedIn and YouTube are their channels. These are the avenues to ingratiate you into their world.

- **Gen Y are huge multi-taskers.**
  They can and will text, check email etc while
  you are presenting or speaking with them, and it
  doesn't mean they are not listening or don't value
  what you have to offer. They may even be taking
  notes on their mobile device, so don't be offended
  and peg them as rude.

Understanding your customers will make all of the
difference in the world in your rate of success.

Take Action – *Make a concerted effort to truly
understand your customer. Before every meeting create
a VIP sheet on your prospect so that you are prepared
and have a clear understanding of whom they are.*

ZZZZZZZZ

**(Now, rest and remember Success is
never final, but a Journey.)**

Rest is as important as the action steps highlighted in this book. We are a society encouraged to work hard, and there is a degree of boastfulness regarding how many hours we work. Rest is, however, equally important as hard work. If we do not fill our tank and are left energy-depleted, our road to success is lengthened.

Rest, refuel, regroup and you will feel refreshed and your effort towards success will be more fruitful and more enjoyable.

> **Take Action –** *Make rest as much a priority as work.*

APPENDIX A

As mentioned throughout this book, the first step towards creating a blueprint of success for your life is to identify your personal four core values. Below is a list of words that will guide you in identifying what values are most important to you. Take your time as you read through the words and circle those words that resonate with who you are. Refrain from circling words that you feel compelled to choose based on what you think other people expect of you. This exercise is intended to guide you in creating a vision of what your life should be.

Accountable
Acknowledgment
Active
Adapt
Affinity
Affluence
Agitate
Allegiance
Amusement
Animate
Appease
Assert

Assist
Association
Attachment
Attempt
Authentic
Authority
Aware
Backbone
Blend
Boost
Brilliance
Brainstorm
Capacity

Captivate

Caring

Caretaker

Challenge

Champion

Charisma

Charm

Chance

Clarify

Class

Collect

Collaborate

Combine

Command

Competent

Composed

Comprehend

Consciousness

Consistent

Consolidate

Conspire

Contribute

Converge

Convince

Coordinate

Counsel

Creative

Credible

Crusade

Cultivate

Curious

Daring

Data

Develop

Devise

Devotion

Devout

Dexterity

Dictate

Discover

Discretion

Discriminate

Disturbance

Dominate

Drive

Earn

Ecstasy

Elation

Embrace

Empower

Enchant

Enhance

Enjoyment

Enterprise

Entertainment

Enthusiasm

Envision

Ethical

Exceed

Exclusive

Expedite

Explore

Expressive	Intrigue
Extreme	Join
Fantasy	Jubilation
Fearless	Kindle
Finesse	Knowing
Flash	Laughter
Flexibility	Lenient
Flux	Light-hearted
Forceful	Love
Fulfill	Loyalty
Fuse	Lucid
Galvanize	Manipulate
Generate	Mentor
Gentleness	Metaphysical
Giggle	Mindful
Give	Motivate
Genuine	Natural
Goodness	Network
Gratification	Observant
Harmonious	Opportunity
Happiness	Peril
Hazard	Persist
Humanity	Pioneer
Impartial	Pious
Implication	Pivot
Impulsive	Prestige
Incite	Process
Individuality	Procedure
Influence	Produce
Insight	Professional
Intention	Progressive

Promote
Propel
Prosperity
Quality
Reciprocate
Refine
Regulate
Reinforce
Relate
Representative
Respectful
Requirements
Revolutionize
Result
Reveal
Reverence
Reward
Riches
Sacred
Safety
Savor

Sensitive
Speculate
Splendor
Stamina
Start
Stimulating
Study
Sustenance
Symmetry
Sympathetic
Territory
Thin-skinned
Thorough
Tranquility
Train
Trustworthy
Vigilant
Vision
Wit

A-Z Blueprint for Success